SECOND NATURE

CITY GALLERY, WELLINGTON, NEW ZEALAND

SECOND NATURE

PETER PERYER, PHOTOGRAPHER, NEW ZEALAND

EDITED BY GREGORY BURKE AND PETER WEIERMAIR

*E*DITION *S*TEMMLE

CONTENTS

PREFACE **PETER WEIERMAIR**

The present volume contains reproductions of 60 photographs by the New Zealand photographer Peter Peryer. Each is presented in isolation in order to emphasise its singularity. All of the photographs reproduced here were taken during the period between 1975 and 1994. Both the editors of the book and the artist himself speak of a "selection", for the life's work of the 44-year-old Peter Chanel Peryer, who came quite late to photography at the age of 32, is much more extensive.

It is important to realise one thing: Peryer himself has developed a core selection of photographs chosen over and over for his exhibitions, and he augments it only gradually and hesitantly. Again and again he examines the meaning and the relevance of these few photographs closely, as if surveying reality, clarifying his assessment of the central images of his "autobiography".

Unlike many other contemporary photographers, Peryer proceeds with caution, deliberately making only few photographs, which he then adds to the existing core. Thus it is not entirely incorrect to refer to the present selection as t h e photographic work of the New Zealand photographer Peter Peryer.

The appeal of Peryer´s photographs derives from the fact that they have the effect of first but at the same time of last, and final, pictures. And what does that mean?

In most cases, the pictures communicate their own content. Sometimes he creates puzzle images, playing with meanings. The majority of his photographs are devoted to the subject of the animate and inanimate nature of his homeland: there are images of plants and animals, characteristic features of the landscape, demarcations of the land and seascape, isolated houses or simple playthings. All subjects are rendered – no, portrayed would be the more appropriate expression – in solid objectivity, almost like pictures in an illustrated lexicon of the country. The term "portrait" seems more suitable because these are laconic, melancholy, isolated and enigmatic portraits of objects important to life in general and to personal life, things which have exercised a decisive influence upon Peryer´s consciousness and his personal history, things that have played, with an intensified, almost symbolic effect, a significant role in the biography of the country itself. It takes courage to portray what has already been rendered so often before. In literature, we are familiar with the movement of concretist poetry, in which language was subjected to a process of purification. Peryer seems to have something similar in mind with his photographs of simple objects of everyday reality.

In his essay, Gregory Burke interprets the iconographic undercurrents and the particular national semantics of many of the elements of Peryer´s pictorial language. He also calls attention to the breadth of Peryer´s knowledge, as a photographer familiar with the history of photographic modernism as well as of the various functions of photography in its non-artistic forms (such as scientific photography).

For Peryer, oppositions such as nature/culture and nature/civilization, but foremostly the opposition between the natural and the artificial, are tensions reflected repeatedly in his work. He does not employ the medium naively, like the photographers of the 19th century, but plays instead with its capacity to create illusion. Objects seem real which are in fact only imitations. In one photograph, a standing puddle of water in the shape of New Zealand is rendered to suggest an aerial photograph of the country. The question of reality and truth in photography are posed again and again in a playful manner.

Of central importance is Peryer´s intention to create a few compelling archetypal images that go beyond the careless verbosity of contemporary photography – to create photographs as complex as good poems, which can be read again and again, and always differently.

SECOND NATURE **GREGORY BURKE**

At the age of 21 Peter Peryer changed his middle name from Ross to Chanel, after Saint Peter Chanel the first Christian martyr of Oceania and to date the only Catholic saint to have lived in New Zealand. In his youthful claim for identity Peryer would have realised that 1941, the year of his own birth, was the centenary of the martyrdom of his namesake. He may also have pondered the significance of the 1840s in terms of the arrival of the Christian missionaries prior to that decade and the subsequent signing of the Treaty of Waitangi in 1840 by chiefs of the indigenous Maori tribes and a representative of the British Crown. It was this treaty that paved the way for the European colonisation of New Zealand. It is unlikely though that Peryer would have considered the significance of the 1840s in relation to the history of the invention of photography. For it was not until he was in his early 30s and after he had rejected his Catholic upbringing that Peryer took up a career as a photographer.

These introductory facts are not offered as an attempt to mythologise Peryer, a photographer who in many ways leads an ordinary life in Auckland, the city of his birth. Rather they register a set of coincidences that suggest a frame of reference for investigating both the New Zealandness and the internationality of Peryer's photographs. This frame of reference links the personal and the social, the local and the global.

Further it suggests an intertwinement between the history of European colonisation in New Zealand and the history of the medium of photography. These connections are important for Peryer, an interest born out in his work. For while the content of his photographs often appears symbolic of an idea of New Zealand – sheep, cows, beaches, native ferns, volcanic cones, etc, the images themselves refer to significant moments in the history of the photographic medium.

This dialogue with photographic history in Peryer's work begins with the nineteenth century and the interest of that age to image people and new terrains; to provide photographic evidence of the unknown, both in terms of emerging psychological investigations and in terms of the documentation of natural wonders and distant cultures. Peryer's work also has a special relationship with the modernism and utopianism of twentieth century photographers such as Edward Weston and László Moholy-Nagy. Of equal importance to Peryer's work is a diverse field of photographic imagery that is largely anonymous; unauthored images that remain undervalued in the published histories of photography. Included here is the photography of animals in the scientific as well as the personal and familial sense; to the photography associated with surveillance, tourism, travel, the family album and the study of topography, geomorphology and botany. The merging of the photographic qualities of such imagery with his own images gives Peryer's work its edge, its ineffability. His photographs not only bear witness to Moholy-Nagy's assertion that photography has changed human perception, but in their very hybridity they provide an idiosyncratic counterpoint to much contemporary photography, photography that engages with a post-modernist investigation of the codes of visual representation.

In notes to an exhibition in 1978 Peryer commented "My photographs are self-portraits. The photographs are somehow related to my past. I don't know why or how".[1] It is still useful to think of Peryer's photographs as self-portraits even though latterly his images appear preoccupied by ordinary objects and are often characterised by a sense of detachment. Certainly in the 1970s portraiture, including self-portraiture, was a hallmark of his identity as a photographer. These were not photographs taken on the run, but rather carefully considered and composed images of himself, his wife Erika Parkinson and close friends. Rather than seeking to probe the essentiality of human character these images exuded a timelessness and appeared more concerned with the elusiveness and theatre of identity.

Peryer portrayed himself in a number of psychological guises: as a naked man holding a rabbit, as a drowned man, as a hos-

1 *Snaps News* 3 Auckland, New Zealand 1978

pitalised patient, as provincial and agrarian. While these works established a typological interest in the human persona they also drew on photographic precursors. *Self-Portrait with Rooster* 1977 (Plate 1) provides a potent example of this. In terms of its treatment of content and its frontal confrontation between subject and camera it is reminiscent of earlier twentieth century images such as *Young Boy, Gondeville, Charente, France* 1951 by the American photographer Paul Strand. Both images are tightly framed and focus on the social position of their subjects connoted by the figures' clothes and their immediate surroundings. But while we are encouraged to locate the subjects in terms of their agricultural occupation, in both cases the intensity of their gaze resists the scrutiny of the camera and its aim of documentary self revelation.

At its most straightforward Peryer's photograph invites us to speculate on the occasion of its taking, to read the picture as a portrait of an impoverished farmer. But as the title declares the image is of Peryer himself, a photograph he has dressed up for by buying and donning a second hand suit and borrowing the rooster he clutches to his chest. While it is the interplay between the rooster, the formality of the suit and the resolute stare of the subject that is both compelling and disconcerting, the use of masquerade gives his image a further twist, for it complicates the tensions between subjectivity and objectivity that are already inherent in self-portraiture. Such contrivance again disturbs the seeming documentary intention of the photograph and gives force to the layers of contradiction contained within the image.

For the photograph concerns itself ultimately with contradiction, an ambivalence symbolically conveyed by the rooster, the animal Peryer identifies with in his dual roles as both subject and photographer. As a farm animal the rooster could allude to Peryer's rural upbringing. However its central and dynamic position within the image gives it the iconographic significance of an attribute of Peryer's persona. Commonly thought of as a symbol of transition, specifically between darkness and light, the rooster is also often used to symbolise masculine prowess. Within Christian iconography the rooster can also act as an attribute of the apostle Saint Peter, an allusion to the crowing cock that signalled the saint's triple denial of Christ. While Peryer empowers his image with such symbolic associations, he amends and constrains them by presenting the rooster with its legs tied. In so doing Peryer simultaneously acknowledges and resists a personal association with the rooster's symbolic inheritance.

The suggestion that Peryer may be identifying with Saint Peter in this image is reinforced by the vague outline of a cross that emerges from the wall behind him. Precedents for the impersonation of biblical figures in photographic portraiture go back at least to F. Holland Day who had himself photographed in the 1890s as the crucified Christ. This is now a tradition continued most recently by French photographers Pierre et Gilles who, in the early 1990s, produced photographs of themselves as saints, a series that included Saint Peter Chanel. However, in their unsettling emotional charge, Peryer's self-portraits have more in common with the photographs taken by the Japanese photographer Eikoh Hosoe of the writer Yukio

elf-Portrait 1977

Mishima in poses of martyred saints. Peryer was unaware of these photographs of Mishima when producing his self-portraits, although he had read and admired his writing[2]. Peryer's self-portraits though, are not strict or singular impersonations. As with *Self-Portrait with Rooster* these images invite both documentary and fantastic interpretations and are thereby rendered timeless.

The portraits Peryer made of others from the 1970s are also characterised by a filmic or theatrical quality. Peryer likened them at the time to film stills[3]. Rather than just seeking to document his subject or to describe his relationship to them Peryer seemed concerned to create images that evoked a feel-

ing, images that explored his psychological relationship both to himself and to photography. Frequently his subjects confronted the camera directly with their gaze as with the portrait of his wife *Erika, Winter 1979* (Plate 3). Typical of many of his portraits this image implies a narrative content closely linked to the photographer, but it also depicts a situation that remains enigmatic for the viewer. This condition of the unknowable

Journey to Wellington from the series *Gone Home* 1975

counteracts the camera's unrelenting and investigative focus on the subject. The duality that is implicit here is conveyed not only by the resolute expression of the subject but also by her hand that seems to float before her chest while it grips and secures her coat. If this ambiguous gesture provides shelter from the weather it also defends the subject from the predatory inquisition of the camera. While signalling both vulnerability and resistance the hand simultaneously offers the potential of revelation.

This restricted concentration on an individual set in isolation is characteristic of Peryer's early work. While portraits were his main activity at this time, Peryer also photographed buildings and domestic interiors. The same sense of seclusion and

2 Barr, Jim 'Peter Peryer' *Photo-Forum Supplement* 1 Summer, Wellington, New Zealand, 1978, p14 (interview)
3 ibid, p13

remoteness carried through into these images. Most often the structures he photographed stood alone in a landscape and were treated as surrogates for human subjects and their social and personal relationship to the world. Again these images are imbued with an intense psychological resonance, many seeming to emerge out of darkness as if from memory. But frequently they also project a wistfulness and whimsicality, qualities that have become an enduring feature of Peryer's work. Take for example *The Divided House* 1975 (Plate 5). This house appears ready to move. Its sentinel perch just shy of the top of the hill enhances the human attributes of its façade. Such impishness is belied by the drama of its central division, a cut that invites us to think of psychological rupture or familial discord. It is however the tension between these generalised interpretations and the particularities and ordinariness of the house itself that activates the image. This is after all a simple suburban bungalow. In itself its façade is uneventful except for the disordered symmetry of the two sets of window frames, an oddity that is accentuated by the divide. It is the attention to such details, to the acute observation of moments of irrationality within mundane situations, that so frequently compels and sustains interest in Peryer's images.

By 1980 Peryer had begun moving away from portraiture in the strict sense. Since then he has ranged widely in his subject matter, photographing many aspects of the natural world – animals, plant forms, landscape, as well as the man-made and processed environment – buildings, boats, monuments. Coincident with this diversification, Peryer renounced the expressionistic, paring right back the emotional content of his work. Having eschewed the dramatic effects created by contrast, his prints became lighter and are now characterised by a predominance of mid-tones. If this was a shift away from what had become conventional in art-photography, so was his increasing focus on the uncelebrated aspects of the everyday. Images of domesticated animals for example have rarely entered the canon of art-photography.

But underlying this apparent pre-occupation with the quotidian, is a set of wide-ranging interests that fuel Peryer's vision of the extraordinary within the commonplace. These include an interest in new developments in physics, an interest in the inter-relationships between botany, biology and cosmology, a particular interest in the natural and social histories of New Zealand, and a long-standing concern for the natural environment. If in one sense Peryer is "telling my personal story in my work"[4] his personal passions are restrained, while his observation remains acute. For finally, all these concerns are framed by an unrelenting interest in photography, both its history and its current ubiquity.

4 Unpublished interview with author, Wellington, New Zealand, 1994

Peryer's change of approach in the 1980s can be seen in his treatment of the human figure. Images such as *Legs* 1980 (Plate 7), *Torso* 1980 (Plate 8) and *Michael Dunn* 1983 (Plate 9) isolate parts of the body and are formally composed, as if inanimate. A response to these photographs shifts between a perception of the rhythmic and emblematic qualities of the total image and a knowledge of the organic and animate nature of the subject matter. In this sense they suggest the influence of modernist photographers such as Weston. Peryer's previous exploration of his psychological relationship to the subject has been disengaged, evidenced by his self-image *Torso* which resists identification by excluding the head. This move to depersonalise and distance the photograph from the reality it documents was amplified by Peryer through his first presentation of *Torso* as a multiple set of 5 prints. In so doing Peryer acknowledged the instrumentality of the photographic process.

The precedence of Modernism continued to inform much of Peryer's work of the 1980s. Its influence is evident in *Frozen Flame* 1982 (Plate 13) with the triangulation of the picture plane, a feature that is echoed in the later work *Trout* 1987 (Plate 27). But more than being simply photographs made in the manner of an earlier model, such images are complicated and thereby activated by reference to multiple sources. *Frozen*

Flame for example, with its down-turned point of view and the planar dissection of its internal elements, is strongly reminiscent of images by Moholy-Nagy of the 1920s and 30s. The title, however, is a direct reference to the New Zealand painting *Frozen Flames* 1931 by Christopher Perkins. This painting depicts the withered branches of a dead tree, set within a brooding and unpeopled landscape. Images of dead or slain trees were com-

Christopher Perkins *Frozen Flames* 1931, oil on canvas. Courtesy of the Auckland City Art Gallery, Auckland, New Zealand

mon in New Zealand painting of this period and were used to symbolise ideas of place, progress, and "man alone" in a new world. They are a reminder that New Zealand from the 1930s through to the 1960s was still very much a pioneer country concerned with organising its landscape as a utility and with pushing through its roading networks. This was the New Zealand of Peryer's childhood, a memory he returns to frequently as a source in his work.

The heroic spirit of the pioneer is specifically and ironically alluded to in his recent image

Eric Lee-Johnson *Country Library Service Bus* 1955, silver gelatin print. Courtesy Auckland City Art Gallery, Auckland, New Zealand

Meccano Bus 1993 (Plate 53) which shows in model form a 1950s bus toiling its way through a landscape recently scarred by earth-moving equipment. However, the pathos conveyed

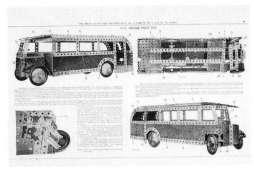

Meccano instructions for making a model bus

by the image is burlesqued by the fact that the bus is made out of Meccano, a kit-set for making models that for many New Zealanders is synonymous with a childhood in suburbia. References to suburbia also pervade *Frozen Flame*. For while Peryer quotes and merges two distinct modernist traditions in this image, one rooted in the international and urban, the other in the nationalistic and the rural, the image itself depicts a suburban garden. Its broken kerbside suggests a struggle to maintain order, a detail that could also suggest the breakdown of a utopian ideal epitomised by suburbia.

Through his interpolation of mundane subject matter into formalist photographic studies, Peryer evokes a quiet sense of both irony and unease. This feature of his work is pronounced in the suite of images *Doughnuts* 1983, *Neenish Tarts* 1983 and *Jam Rolls* 1983 (Plates 14, 15, 16). The tilted picture plane in these images, combined with the interest in geometric order and repetition, reprises visual strategies associated with constructivist photography. But these are not however images of organic or mechanistic forms composed within the frame to communicate a progressive vision. Rather, the multiple units in these pictures are mass-produced cakes, subtle reminders of standardised social behaviour. This translation of production-line food into high art introduces a levity into the images which counteracts their more disquieting aspects, their allusion to social regimentation and restriction and the darker sides of normality.

There is also a strong emblematic character to such images, a quality that is redoubled through an association of their subject matter with time and place. This aspect of Peryer's work is particularly evident in *Kiokio* 1984 and *Piupiu* 1984 (Plates 17 and 18), the fern being a national emblem of New Zealand. Many of his other subjects have also been standard-bearers of national identity; the sheep in *Farm Study* 1986 (Plate 19) for example or the snow-capped peaks in *Mountain Scene* 1988 (Plate 31). The meaning of the photograph *Sea Elephant* 1989 (Plate 33) is partly determined by the promotion of New Zealand internationally as an environmental haven, while *Kangaroos* 1987 (Plate 23) depicts a popular Australian icon. If such photographs depict clichés the images themselves are multivalent and thereby ambiguous. The subject of *Sea Elephant* for example is treated as if it were human following the traditions of photographic portraiture. And in *Mountain Scene*, the drama and majesty of the mountain range, a feature typical of the promotional imagery of New Zealand's scenery, is subdued by the flattening of the picture plane. The muting of the tonal range links the image to the landscape photographs Peryer has studied in books of New Zealand geomorphology. And yet, by means of the title, Peryer also reinforces a connection to the tradition of the picturesque. Stylistic associations such as these have the effect of distancing Peryer's images from the present. This is due not just to the treatment of the overall image but often to the pro-perties of the subject itself, as can be seen in *The Alexandra Clock* 1988 (Plate 30). While the hands of this clock point to an undated time of 5.47, the styling of its dial insinuates a moment in the 1950s. Maximised by Peryer's decision to restrict his prints to black and white, the dated effect of his images reorders the value his subjects have as symbols of place, while also parodying the "decisive moment", an ideal advanced within the modernist tradition of documentary photography.

Queenstown and the Remarkables,
The Alexandra Clock and
Model Pa at Whakarewarewa,
from the Peryer post-card collection

A strong sense of familiarity is intrinsic to much of Peryer's work. In their quotation of multiple styles of picture-making his photographs parade their status and historical meaning as images. But often his images only mimic the familiar, offering a layer of disguise that forces his audience to review first impressions. An apt example of this is *New Zealand 15.3.1991* (Plate 46). Here we have a map of Peryer's homeland, the ulti-mate symbol of nationality. In its graininess and aerial view it reads as if taken from a satellite, a fiction encouraged by the title's rigorous dating of the image. Such impressions are illu-sory, disturbed by the texture and sharp focus of the concrete surface on which the map is painted.

Images such as these are uncanny. Frequently the viewer is left unsure of the reality they depict, whether their subjects are models or life size, as in *Engine Leaving Glen Innes Tunnel* 1992 (Plate 51) or *Home* 1991 (Plate 52); or of the distance of the subject from the camera, as in *Black Nerita* 1986 (Plate 20) or *One Tree Hill* 1992 (Plate 45). When presented together this sense of uncertainty carries over into seemingly more straight-forward photographs.

An air of artificiality lingers in the image *Street Scene, Oamaru* 1988 (Plate 28) for example. Its historic architecture and absence of people makes it reminiscent of the Parisian street scenes photographed by Charles Marville in the 1860s or

Eugène Atget in the 1900s and in this sense Peryer's image feels out of time. This street in Oamaru has been declared historic, sign-posted as photogenic. As a scene it emanated a deep sense of nostalgia before Peryer arrived with his camera, an already established transformation of meaning that heightens the irreality of his image.

Intrinsic to the experience of much of Peryer's work is this transposition of subject matter, the sense of a quiver between the real and the artificial, the banal and the sublime. It is crucial to the reception of *Dead Steer* 1987 (Plate 24) for instance. This photograph not only documents the recent death of a farm animal but also records its transformation into an image. This is finally the point, for once again the subject's status as an image appears to have preceded the taking of the photograph. However unwittingly, this animal's comic artificiality was imposed at the point of death, a fact that gives Peryer's photograph a macabre twist. It is an effect that is echoed in *Trap* 1992 (Plate 47). In this case though, the animal's death and subsequent transformation into an image or still life, was premeditated by Peryer and pre-visualised by the manufacturers of the trap. For it was an illustrated advertisement for the device that motivated Peryer to make the photograph. This frisson, between the animate and the inanimate, between the mobile and the stationary, also activates images such as *The*

Concrete Rabbit 1982 (Plate 10) or *Sand Shark* 1991 (Plate 44). Such images parody the irreality produced by the photographic process through its freezing and composing of time. It is finally Peryer's playfulness with this fundamental aspect of photography that links his images of both the real and the imaginary. Since its inception photography has played an important part in determining the collective memory, in historicising events. As markers of places, occasions or people, photographs frequently act as souvenirs. An awareness of this fact strongly influenced the use of photography in the latter half of the nineteenth century. Consequently images associated with travel figure strongly in the photography of this period. The touring photographer of this age was frequently attracted to the exotic – to giant trees in distant forests, to wild animals such as alligators, to natural wonders such as waterfalls or to the alien architecture of distant cultures.

Peryer references this tradition in images such as *Kauri* 1993 (Plate 57), *Alligator* 1988 (Plate 32), *Waterfall* 1982 (Plate 12) and *Whakarewarewa* 1993 (Plate 54). But while these images suggest an interest in the history associated with travel, they are also attuned to the transformation of meaning of the subjects through the advent of contemporary tourism. Such subjects are now already souvenirs, collected and managed in relation to a tourist economy, an economy that is dependant on photography. They circulate as images in family albums, in tourist brochures or as postcards. As such they are known and previsualised prior to the arrival of the tourist. And they are managed for the ease of photography. The kauri tree and the waterfall are conveniently located on tourist routes, the alligator is kept at a safe distance in a zoo, while the model pah has been built for the purpose, its authenticity amended by its history as a feature of a tourist village.

The photography connected to tourism is an important source for many of Peryer's images as evidenced by his collection of postcards. These images layer many of his photographs with extra significance and in this sense they become a subject of his work in their own right. But his photographs are never

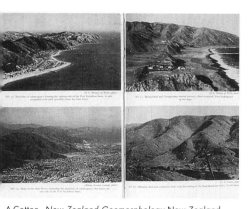

A Cotton, *New Zealand Geomorphology* New Zealand
niversity Press, Wellington, New Zealand 1955
lates xiv, xv

straight copies. His translation of tourist imagery from colour to black and white is one way of ensuring this. And again his photographs are frequently loaded with multiple references to the history of photography. *Westhaven* 1989 (Plate 40) is a pertinent example of this, a curious hybrid. For three photographic sources dominate this work. There is

an affinity with the formalism of Moholy-Nagy and in particular his image *Boats in the Old Port of Marseilles* 1929, a reference also to postcard imagery of the same scene, and finally an allusion to the topographical concerns and approach of aerial photography. And of course the image is once again an emblem, the boats themselves being a metaphor for travel as well as being an allusion to both the history and current aspirations of New Zealand as a nation of travellers.[5]

For Peryer tourism and travel are not necessarily the same thing. His work acknowledges the travel associated with natural history, with science, with the imperatives of topography. However Peryer highlights interconnections between travel and tourism through their mutual relationship to the history of the photographic medium. His work tells us that in the late twentieth century photographic imagery often precedes experience. But while he acknowledges the partiality and artificiality of the photographic process, he asserts its continuing potential to examine the detail of the everyday. By amending and displacing the familiar, Peryer reaffirms a faith in photography and its enduring power to tell us something of who and where we are.

5 This multicultural history is wryly alluded
to in the image *Edward Bullmore's Launch* 1993 (Plate 55),
and specifically in *Marsden Cross* 1994 (Plate 56),
which is an image of the monument to the first Christian service
and first European birth in New Zealand.

SACRED FIRE **HELEN ENNIS**

There was a rock that since the creation

of the world had been worked upon

by the pure essences of Heaven and the fine savours

of Earth, the vigour of sunshine and the grace

of moonlight, till at last it became magically

pregnant . . .[1]

Whenever I see photographs by Peter Peryer I feel that they are looking at me. The connections are as strong and unexpected as that. I am physically struck by their resoluteness or "thereness" as well as the energy which flows beyond their borders. So I stop, leaving aside for a moment the hurly burly of daily life. A conversation begins, with many gentle twists and turns and no ending; our topic is huge – "life" in its most general sense. For Peryer's photographs are explorations into being alive rather than documents or records of contemporary life.

At their heart lies Peter Peryer's relation to the world: Emile Zola's famous definition of art – "Nature as seen through a temperament" – holds true. One sees in Peryer's work a knitting together of the powers of observation and empathy, a gentle union of science and art. The process is remarkably uncomplicated and precise. An image like *Janet's Hand* 1993 (Plate 49) is stunning in its clarity; the composition pivots on the won-

1 Wu Ch'eng-en, *Monkey* (translated from the Chinese by Arthur Waley), London: George Allen & Unwin, 1953, p11.

derfully dynamic interplay of just three elements – forearm, hand and wall.

Moeraki Boulder 1988 (Plate 25) too uses a finely tuned visual language. Sky, sea, foam and stone are wedded to each other, each with a part to play. But it is the solitary boulder whose presence is inescapable. Wherever you look without a fuss it draws in your eye.

The boulder's attraction could be explained in compositional terms; positioned slightly off-centre, it gives the picture its marvellous balance and asymmetry, the perfection of a Japanese garden. Its rounded form evokes pleasurable associations: water and weather-worn smooth, it is semi-circular like a rising or setting sun, whale-like with black, weighty flanks that crest above the sea-water. Also satisfying is its materiality, in the midst of never-ending flux it alone is solid and still. There it stands, age-old, an emblem of nature and, in its evocation of a neolithic monument, a symbol of civilisation.

While such analyses are seductive they fall far short of explaining the effect of a photograph such as *Moeraki Boulder*. And so, I find myself in another realm, one which calls up a different language perhaps better suited to evoking a boulder's life. For the Moeraki boulder is not inanimate. If it had eyes and could see me I would not be surprised. Such phenomena are not unusual in Peter Peryer's photographs; acts of transub-stantiation come about simply, without strain or excess. The commonplace becomes extraordinary, "non-living" things like flecks of sea-foam, a sand sculpture and a model house attain a heightened reality, and animals and birds become like us.

Look at the tiny seed pod in *Wattle* 1987 (Plate 22) which swims through the air like a transparent little fish, a sperm or a whitebait whose insides shine through silvery skin. In closeup as under a microscope its features are lovingly revealed. Its eye is big and round with wonderment and its chin curves gently upwards hinting at a smile.

Anthropomorphism is not the point. The "thingness" of Peter Peryer's subjects is respected – indeed, loved. Peryer's world is not divided into the human and non human, the living and the dead, the superior and the inferior. The nature of the species or substances photographed is not an issue – animals, birds, people, natural and made things, all are given the same rapt attention.

The bond between Peter Peryer and those he photographs has all the intensity of a one-to-one relationship. Moods vary – sometimes playful, melancholic, sometimes joyful – but the commitment is unwavering. Compassion and respect are guiding principles, subjects are never belittled, brutalised and turned into spectacle.

Once solitariness spelt loneliness in Peryer's photographs. Now it stands for strength. A single subject is invariably the focus, freed from the distractions and noisy, competing claims of crowds and groups. The Moeraki boulder is alone, away from its invisible seawater and sand-bound companions, while the seedpod hangs from its unseen tree by a slender, twiggy umbilical cord. There is nothing to blur the sightlines leading us to the centre points of these photographs, nothing to disrupt the energy that emanates from them.

The distinctive pulse of *Moeraki Boulder* can be easily heard: it is a kind of music that calmly, quietly engenders a contemplative even meditative response. *Wattle* has yet another beat, whispering rapturously of love.

1 **Self-Portrait with Rooster** 1977

2 **My Parents** 1979

3 **Erika, Winter** 1979

4 **Hunua** 1975

5 **Divided House** 1975

6 **Erika** 1982

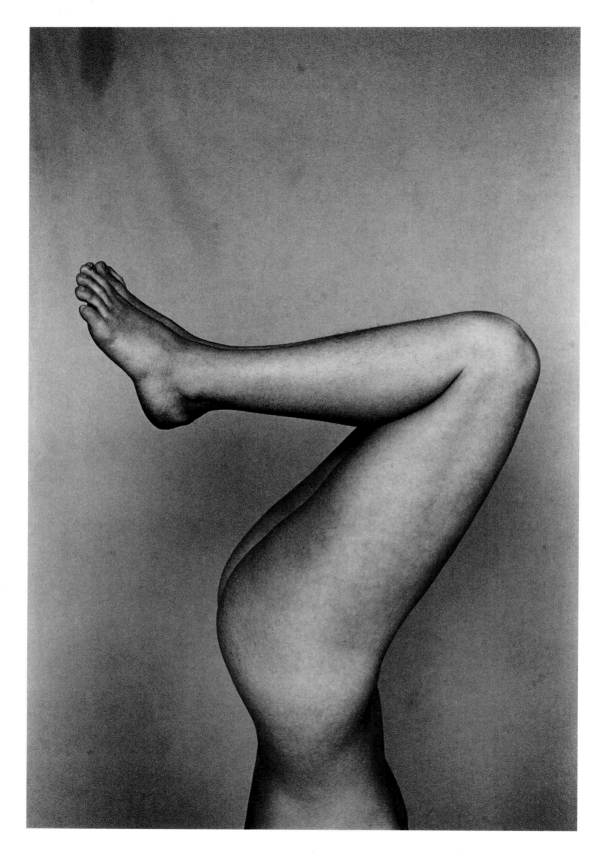

7 **Legs** 1980

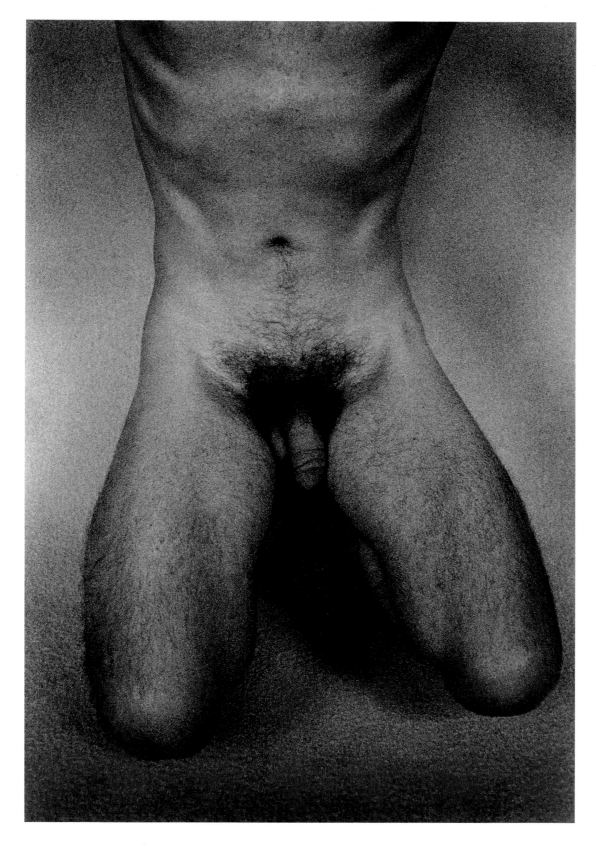

8 **Torso** 1980

9 **Michael Dunn** 1983

10 **The Concrete Rabbit** 1982

11 **Ngaruawahia** 1981

12 **Waterfall** 1982

13 **Frozen Flame** 1982

14 **Doughnuts** 1983

15 **Neenish Tarts** 1983

16 **Jam Rolls** 1983

17 **Kiokio** 1984

18 **Piupiu** 1984

19 **Farm Study** 1986

20 **Black Nerita** 1986

21 **Octopus** 1985

22 **Wattle** 1987

23 **Kangaroos** 1987

24 **Dead Steer** 1987

25 **Moeraki Boulder** 1988

26 **Pouerua** 1988

27 **Trout** 1987

28 **Street Scene, Oamaru** 1988

29 **St Bathans** 1988

31 **Mountain Scene** 1988

33 **Sea Elephant** 1989

34 **Rosie** 1988

35 **Wandering Albatross** 1989

36 **Rockhopper Penguin** 1989

37 **Yellow Eyed Penguin** 1989

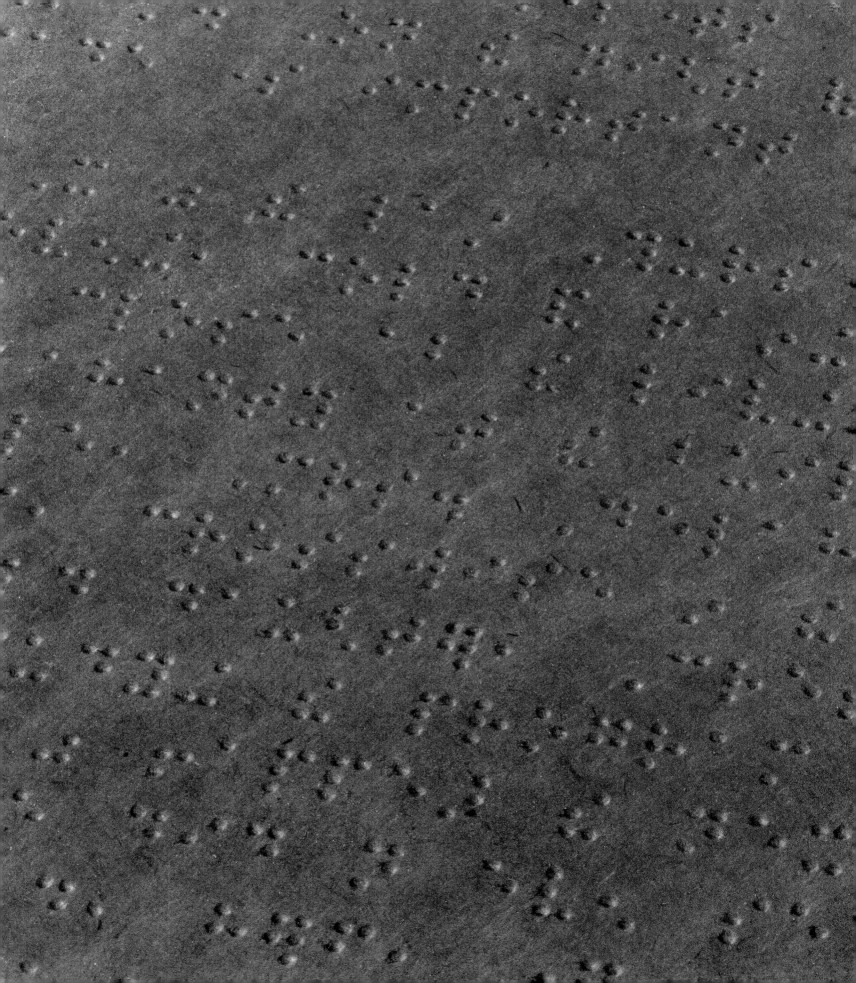

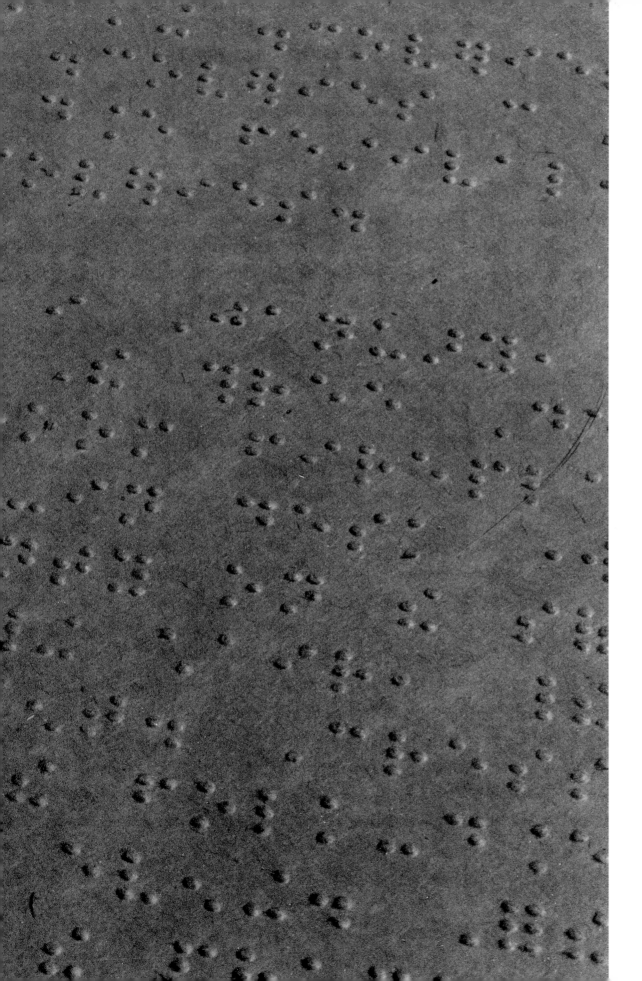

39 **Ruapehu** 1990

40 **Westhaven** 1989

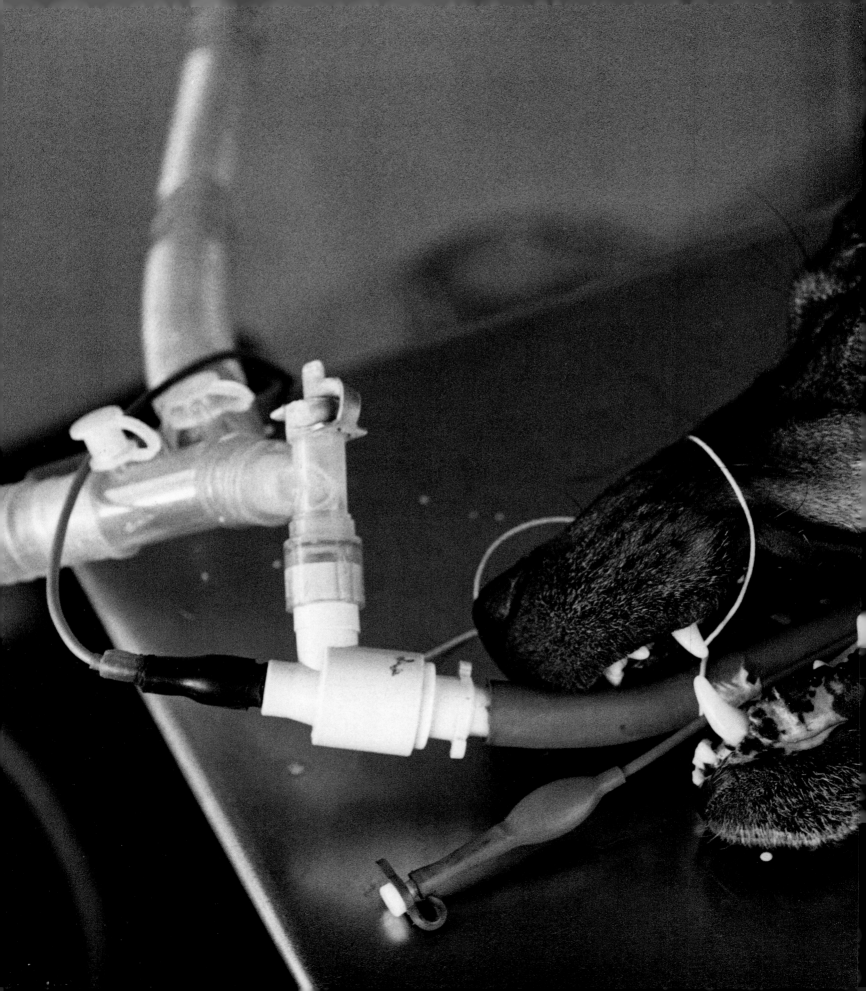

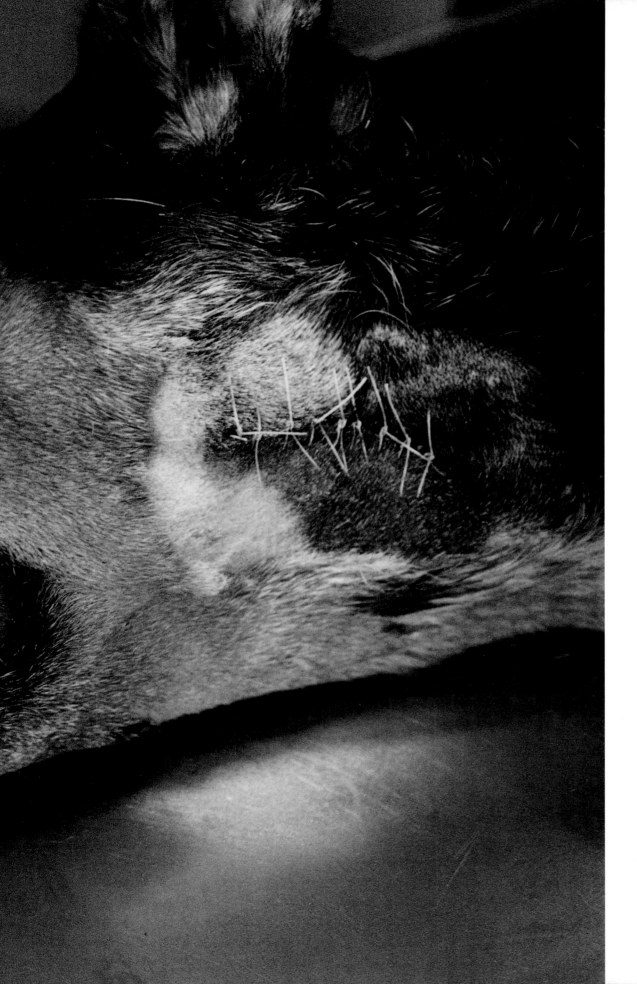

41 **Dog Head** 1990

43 **Spindrift** 1991

44 **Sand Shark** 1991

45 **One Tree Hill** 1992

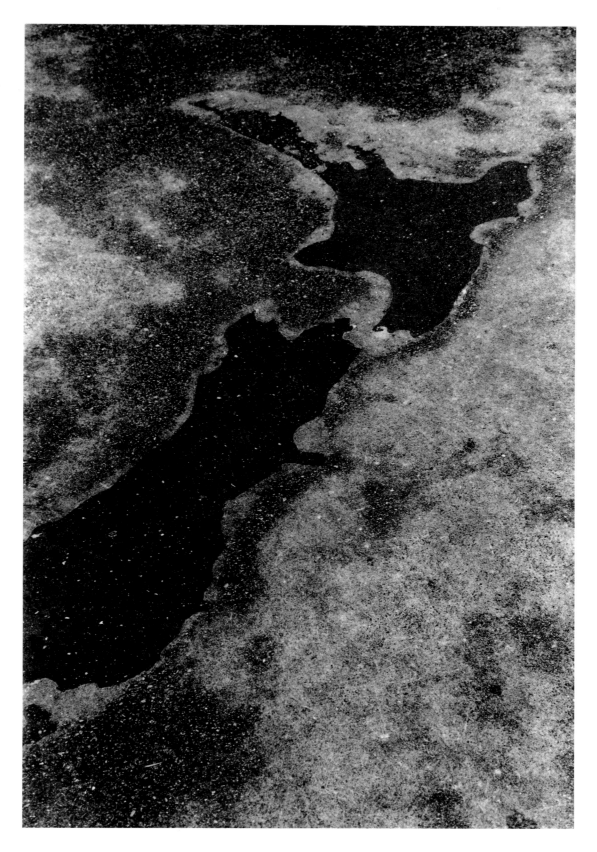

46 **New Zealand** 15.3.1991

47 **Trap** 1992

48 **Tine** 1993

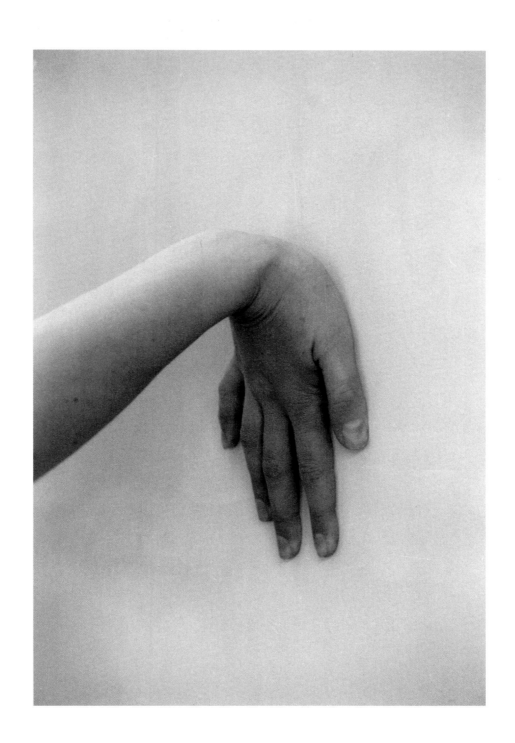

49 **Janet's Hand** 1993

51 **Engine Leaving Glen Innes Tunnel** 1992

54 **Whakarewarewa** 1993

55 **Edward Bullmore's Launch** 1993

56 **Marsden Cross** 1994

57 **Kauri** 1993

58 **Trig** 1993

59 **Ragnarok** 1994

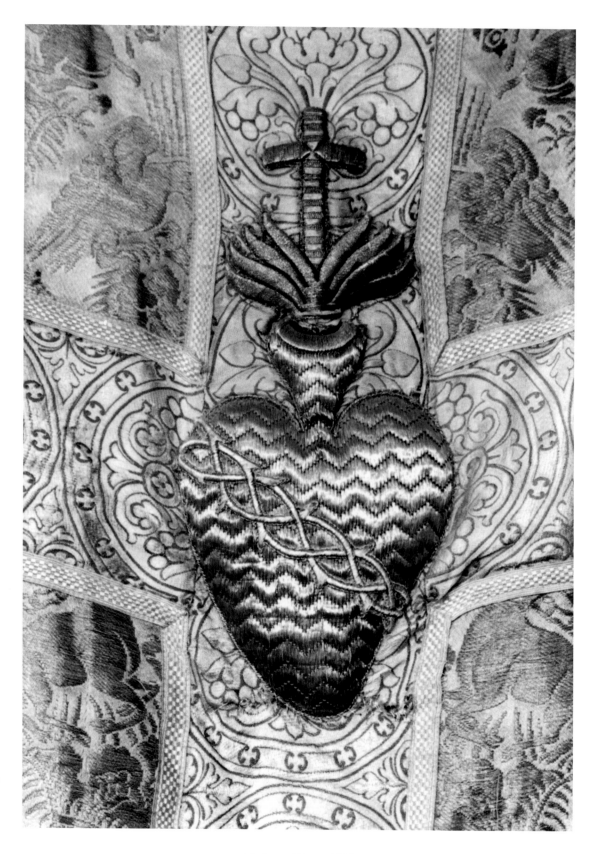

60 **Sacred Heart** 1993

Born in Auckland, New Zealand in 1941, Peter Chanel Peryer is of English, Irish, and Welsh extraction. On his maternal side his family have been in New Zealand for several generations. The name Peryer (rhymes with merrier) is an old English name meaning dweller by the pear tree. In his early twenties he chose Chanel as his middle name reflecting the rigorous Catholic upbringing that he received. By his mid-twenties, Peryer had turned his back on Christianity, and has never returned.

Raised mainly in the Far North of his country, in a sparsely populated, predominantly Maori area, his parents owned small hotels and dairy farms. Being the days before the proliferation of a tourist industry in New Zealand, these hotels always had guests, many of whom were a major influence on Peryer's life. For example, a troupe of travelling entertainers who regularly used the hotel as their base and with whom he formed a deep personal connection. Judges, priests, commercial travellers, school inspectors, these were some of the colourful individuals who peopled his early years.

A hill near one of his homes was the site of a New Zealand equivalent of Little Big Horn. Here, at Ohaeawai, in 1845, the British suffered a major loss.

Right behind his school was a large rock, Taiamai, upon which the souls of dead Maori were said to rest during their journey to the Underworld. Surrounding Ohaeawai are a number of exquisite, extinct volcanic cones. These cones, the site of hundreds of years of human occupation, were visited by Charles Darwin during the voyage of the Beagle. A photograph of one of these, *Pouerua* 1988, appears on plate 26.

Guns and tractors, deep pools, ocean shores, thermal lakes, dogs, horses, birds and fish, American movies, swamps, milking sheds, wood sheds, and the Mass; all of these are sources from which so many of his images are drawn.

After studying both science and the humanities at University Peryer spent several years teaching at Primary, Secondary and Tertiary levels until, at the age of 32, he, seemingly quite suddenly, never having owned a camera before, decided that photography was his vocation. He swiftly taught himself all the craft that he needed to know in order to get started and his images immediately found a small but appreciative audience.

He lives in Auckland with Erika Parkinson, his wife of 30 years. They have two adult children, Amy and Clovis.

1993 **Sue Crockford Gallery, Auckland, New Zealand;**
Hamish McKay Gallery, Wellington, New Zealand
1992 **Gow Langsford Gallery, Auckland, New Zealand;**
Recent Work **Govett Brewster Art Gallery, New Plymouth, New Zealand**
(toured New Zealand)
1989 **Southern Cross Gallery, Wellington, New Zealand**
1988 **Real Pictures Gallery, Auckland, New Zealand**
1989 **Southern Cross Gallery, Wellington, New Zealand**
1987 **George Fraser Gallery, Auckland, New Zealand**

Peter Peryer Poster,
Dowse Art Museum,
Lower Hutt,
New Zealand 1977,
featuring *Christine
Mathieson* 1977

1985 **Centre for Contemporary Art, Hamilton, New Zealand;**
Peter Peryer/Photographs **Sarjeant Gallery, Wanganui, New Zealand**
(toured New Zealand)
1984 *Peter Peryer/Recent Photographs* **Peter McLeavey Gallery,**
Wellington, New Zealand;
Denis Cohn Gallery, Auckland, New Zealand
1982 **Space, Auckland, New Zealand**
1977 *Peter Peryer: An Introduction* **Dowse Art Museum, Lower Hutt,**
New Zealand
1976 *For Your Pleasure* **Snaps Gallery, Auckland, New Zealand;**
Peter Webb Galleries, Auckland, New Zealand
1975 **Dowse Art Museum, Lower Hutt, New Zealand (with Don Driver)**

1994 *Pictograms* **Monash University Gallery, Victoria, Australia**
(toured Australia)
1992 *Scenes from Real and Imaginary Lives* **Wellington City Art Gallery,**
Wellington, New Zealand
1991 *Pacific Parallels* **San Diego Museum of Art, San Diego, USA**
(toured USA)
175° East **Sarjeant Gallery, Wanganui, New Zealand (toured Australia);**
Headlands – Thinking through New Zealand art **Museum of Contemporary**
Art, Sydney, Australia and Museum of New Zealand Te Papa Tongarewa,
Wellington, New Zealand
1990 *Two Centuries of New Zealand Landscape Art* **Auckland City**
Art Gallery, Auckland, New Zealand
1989 *From Today Painting is Dead* **Shed 11, National Art Gallery,**
Wellington, New Zealand;
Imposing Narratives: Beyond the documentary in recent New Zealand
photography **Wellington City Art Gallery, Wellington, New Zealand**
(toured New Zealand)
1988 **Mezzanine Gallery, New Zealand House, London, UK;**
Seven Photographers' Update **Sarjeant Gallery, Wanganui, New Zealand**
1987 *The Trained Eye* **National Art Gallery, Wellington, New Zealand**

Pictograms exibition
catalogue, Australian
Exhibitions Touring
Agency 1994, featuring
Home 1991

1986 *Content/Context: A survey of recent New Zealand art* Shed 11,
National Art Gallery, Wellington, New Zealand
1985 *Posing a Threat* National Art Gallery, Wellington, New Zealand;
The Word Bishop Suter Art Gallery, Nelson, New Zealand
1984 *Anxious Images: Aspects of recent New Zealand art* Auckland City
Art Gallery, Auckland, New Zealand (toured);
The Chelsea Project Auckland City Art Gallery, Auckland, New Zealand;
The Body in Question National Art Gallery, Wellington, New Zealand
1983 *International Photography 1980-82* National Gallery of Australia,
Canberra (toured Australia)
1982 *Me by Myself: The self-portrait* National Art Gallery, Wellington,
New Zealand;
Views/Exposures: Ten contemporary New Zealand photographers National
Art Gallery, Wellington, New Zealand (toured New Zealand);
Vision in Disbelief: The 4th Biennale of Sydney Art Gallery of New South
Wales, Sydney, Australia;
Time Release Auckland War Memorial Museum, Auckland, New Zealand;
The Nude Exposed Robert McDougall Art Gallery, Christchurch, New Zealand
1979 *Three New Zealand Photographers* Auckland City Art Gallery,
Auckland, New Zealand (toured New Zealand)
1978 *Antipodean Images* New Zealand House, London, UK
1977 *Twenty New Zealand Photographers* Auckland War Memorial
Museum, Auckland, New Zealand
1976 *Photo-Forum '76* Auckland War Memorial Museum, Auckland,
New Zealand
1975 *The Active Eye* Manawatu Art Gallery, Palmerston North,
New Zealand (toured New Zealand)

SELECTED BIBLIOGRAPHY

Barr, Jim 'Peter Peryer' *Photo-Forum Supplement* 1 Summer, Wellington,
New Zealand 1977/78 pp9-15 (interview)
Barr, Jim and Mary Barr *Peter Peryer* Sarjeant Art Gallery Wanganui,
New Zealand 1985
Blackman, Gary 'The photographic experience' *Photo-Forum Supplement*
3 Spring, Wellington, New Zealand 1979 p5
Vision in Disbelief: The 4th Biennale of Sydney Art Gallery of New South
Wales Sydney, Australia 1982 p81

Photo-Forum Calendar
1985, featuring
Tumblers 1984

Bogle, Andrew *Three New Zealand Photographers* Auckland City Art
Gallery, Auckland, New Zealand 1979
'Three New Zealand Photographers' *Photo-Forum Supplement* 3
Spring 1979 p4
Bosworth, Rhondda 'Peter Peryer: In a constant state of change' *Snaps
News* 3, Auckland, New Zealand 1978 p2 (interview)
Burke, Gregory *Imposing Narratives: Beyond the documentary
in recent New Zealand photography* Wellington City Art Gallery,
Wellington, New Zealand 1989 pp13, 62-67
Curnow, Wystan 'New Zealand art – where in the world is it?' *New Zealand
Listener* April 3 1982 pp34-35
Elias, Ann 'Peter Peryer' *Art New Zealand* 53 Summer 1989-90 p80
'Wide ranging images' *New Zealand Listener* March 8 1986 pp34
Eldredge, Charles C. *Pacific Parallels* San Diego Museum of Art, San Diego
U.S.A 1991 pp47-48, 50
Fraser, Ross 'Peter Peryer: The photograph as a portrait of the self'
Art New Zealand 8 November/December 1977 pp25, 65, 67

Headlands – Thinking through New Zealand art Museum of Contemporary Art, Sydney, Australia 1991 pp46, 72

Hurrell, John 'The New Zealand work in the forth biennale of Sydney' *The Bulletin of the Robert McDougall Art Gallery – Supplement* Christchurch, New Zealand July/August 1982

Hutchins, Tom *Photo-Forum* 33 August/September, Wellington, New Zealand 1976 p18

International Photography 1920-1980 National Gallery of Australia, Canberra 1982

Ireland, Peter 'The Significance of repetition' *Art New Zealand* 32 1984 pp34-35

Johnston, Alexa *Anxious Images: Aspects of recent New Zealand art* Auckland City Art Gallery, Auckland, New Zealand 1984 p53-58

Keith, Sheridan 'Frontierland – The Photographs of Peter Peryer' *London Magazine* 21 (4) July 1981 p42-49

'Ten Images' *London Magazine* July 1990

'The Chelsea Project' *Art New Zealand* 34 1985 pp18-21

'A desire to understand' *New Zealand Listener* February 7 1981 p36-37

Kelly, Desmond 'The new image: Twelve contemporary photographers' *Art New Zealand* 13 1979 p61

Main, William and J B Turner *New Zealand Photography since 1840* Photo-Forum, Wellington, New Zealand 1993 pp68-69

Me by Myself: The self-portrait National Art Gallery, Wellington, New Zealand 1982

'Peter Peryer' *Creative Camera International Yearbook* 1978 London pp113-123

'Peter Peryer' *Photo-Forum* 29 December, Wellington, New Zealand 1975 pp10-15 (portfolio with statement)

'Peter Peryer' *Photo-Forum* 33 August/September, Wellington, New Zealand 1976 pp14-17 (portfolio with statement)

'Peter Peryer' *Spleen 7*, Auckland, New Zealand 1977 pp8-13 (portfolio)

Spens, Michael 'Monet not Maori: Art in New Zealand' *Studio International* 198 (1010) 1985 pp50-51

The Active Eye Manawatu Art Gallery Palmerston North, New Zealand 1975 pp82-83

Turner, John 'New Zealand photography since 1945' *Printletter* 23 4:5 September/October, Zurich 1979 pp14-18

Tweedie, Merylyn 'Feminist issues in New Zealand art (with particular reference to imaging of the nude female/the naked woman)' *AGMANZ Journal* 17 (1) Autumn 1986 pp11-12

Views/Exposures: Ten contemporary New Zealand photographers National Art Gallery, Wellington, New Zealand 1982 pp96-105

Wedde, Ian 'A Shark in Time' *Midwest 1* Govett Brewster Art Gallery, New Plymouth, New Zealand 1992 p19

SELECTED PUBLIC COLLECTIONS

Auckland City Art Gallery, Auckland, New Zealand

Bibliothèque Nationale, Paris, France

Dunedin Public Art Gallery, Dunedin, New Zealand

Museum of New Zealand Te Papa Tongarewa, Wellington, New Zealand

National Gallery of Australia, Canberra

Sarjeant Gallery, Wanganui, New Zealand

Waikato Museum of Art and History Te Whare Taonga O Waikato, Hamilton, New Zealand

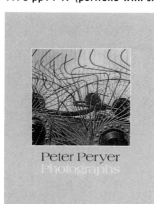

Peter Peryer exhibition catalogue, Sarjeant Gallery, Wanganui, New Zealand 1985, featuring *Hay Tedder* 1985

LIST OF PLATES

27

Trout (Lake Taupo) 1987

405 x 275 mm

28

Street Scene, Oamaru 1988

305 x 460 mm

29

St Bathans (Central Otago) 1988

270 x 410 mm

30

The Alexandra Clock 1988

270 x 410 mm

31

Mountain Scene 1988

275 x 420 mm

32

Alligator 1988

300 x 455 mm

33

Sea Elephant (female) 1989

300 x 455 mm

34

Rosie 1988

265 x 265 mm

35

Wandering Albatross (Auckland Island) 1989

275 x 420 mm

36

Rockhopper Penguin (Campbell Island) 1989

275 x 420 mm

37

Yellow Eyed Penguin (Enderby Island) 1989

275 x 420 mm

38

Seeing 1989

275 x 420 mm

39

Ruapehu 1990

355 x 360 mm

40

Westhaven (Auckland) 1989

480 x 480 mm

41

Dog Head 1990

315 x 470 mm

42

Music 1991

275 x 415 mm

43

Spindrift 1991

200 x 300 mm

44

Sand Shark 1991

275 x 415 mm

45

One Tree Hill 1992

275 x 415 mm

46

New Zealand 15.3.1991

420 x 280 mm

47

Trap 1992

230 x 380 mm

48

Tine 1993

545 x 360 mm

49

Janet's Hand 1993

385 x 250 mm

50

Deer 1993

390 x 440 mm

51

Engine Leaving Glen Innes Tunnel 1992

355 x 355 mm

52

Home 1991

285 x 430 mm

53

The Meccano Bus 1994

360 x 545 mm

54

Whakarewarewa 1993

335 x 505 mm

55

Edward Bullmore's Launch (Lake Tawawera) 1993

415 x 270 mm

56

Marsden Cross 1994

505 x 335 mm

57

Kauri (Tapu Hill) 1993

545 x 360 mm

58

Trig (Rangitoto Island) 1993

535 x 360 mm

59

Ragnarok 1994

360 x 545 mm

60

Sacred Heart 1993

455 x 300 mm

All prints black and white gelatin

The exhibition was organised
in association with the City Gallery, Wellington, New Zealand.
The exhibition has been supported
by the Arts Council of New Zealand / Toi Aotearoa
through its international exchange programme.

Photo reproduction copyright by Peter Peryer
Text copyright by the authors
Translation of the preface from the German by John S. Southard
Art direction and typography by Grafikdesign Peter Wassermann and Andrea Hostettler, Flurlingen, Switzerland
Photolithography by Repro Fuchs GmbH, Salzburg, Austria
Printed and bound by Passavia Druckerei GmbH, Passau, Germany

ISBN 3-905514-56-7